For Zachary, Rufus, Max, Harriet
and Arthur – go to sleep! – I.T.

For Seth, always – S.F.C.

First published in Great Britain in 2021 by Wren & Rook

Text copyright © Isabel Thomas, 2021
Illustration copyright © Stephanie Fizer Coleman, 2021

HB ISBN: 978 1 5263 6257 5
PB ISBN: 978 1 5263 6256 8
E-book ISBN: 978 1 5263 6258 2
10 9 8 7 6 5 4 3 2 1

MIX
Paper from
responsible sources
FSC® C104740

Wren & Rook
An imprint of
Hachette Children's Group
Part of Hodder & Stoughton
Carmelite House
50 Victoria Embankment
London EC4Y 0DZ

An Hachette UK Company
www.hachette.co.uk
www.hachettechildrens.co.uk

Publishing Director: Debbie Foy
Editor: Phoebe Jascourt
Art Director: Laura Hambleton
Designer: Nathalie Eyraud

Printed in China

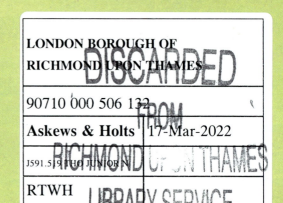

Written by ISABEL THOMAS

Illustrated by STEPHANIE FIZER COLEMAN

Snug Bugs
and
Sleeping
Lions

wren
&rook

When the sun is sinking in the sky and the day is almost done,
do you brush your teeth, snuggle up and share your favourite book?
As the evening fades to darkness and the stars begin to shine,
do you switch off lights, say 'Goodnight' and close your tired eyes?

No matter when or where you sleep,
it's never only you.
Bugs and lions, birds and bears
are feeling sleepy too.

Near a rushing river, along a grassy bank, mallard ducks rest side by side, lined up in a row. They tuck their bills under their downy feathers to keep warm.

In the middle of the huddle, the birds have both eyes tightly closed.
But the ducks at either end sleep with one eye open.
As half their brain dozes the other half stays wide awake,
so they can guard the sleeping group all night long.

On a misty Chinese hillside, a **giant panda** waddles through bamboo, tearing down and munching woody stalks.

Head over heels in a black and white blur, she somersaults down a slope. It's tiring eating grass all day and soon this sleepy bear will need to nap.

A sleepy panda yawns just like a sleepy human!

Pandas can sleep almost anywhere – sprawled on their stomachs,
flopped on their backs or rolled up in a ball. Today she clambers
up a tree and settles on a branch, cushioned by her soft, fluffy fur.

As dusk falls in a dusty African desert, the animals that kept cool in the blazing sun must now work together to keep warm.

One by one, a mob of meerkats disappears underground. Scampering through sandy burrows, they choose a sleeping chamber for the night. Clambering and scrambling with paws over heads over tails, they form a fuzzy pile.

Above ground, chattering and chirping fills the desert. Hundreds of **weaver birds** return to roost in their giant nest – a heavy haystack balanced on the branches of a camel thorn tree. The air is icy, but the birds stay snug under their thatched roof.

Sleeping in a heap will keep them warm and safe!

The sun sinks over a shallow lagoon and the Caribbean sky blushes pink. An enormous flock of **flamingos** wades and paddles, honks and gabbles, squabbling over the best spots. Those that can will doze in the water where they stand.

Could you fall asleep balancing on one leg?

Each flamingo tucks one leg up underneath its body. They lock an ankle, curl their long necks and rest their sleepy heads on their feathery backs.

Just below the surface of the starlit sea, a pod of **sperm whales** prepares to take a nap. Together they rise to the surface, filling their lungs with a great gulp of fresh air. This will have to last until they wake again.

They turn and plunge headfirst back into the water, sinking slowly and silently. Until suddenly they stop. Their bulky bodies flip over and drift up again towards the light.

Together they doze vertically, their huge heads up and tail flukes down. Unaware of every ocean sound, they only wake if something brushes their skin.

The tiniest tickle will wake a whale!

Close to the Alaskan coast, the water ripples and churns
as a group of sea otters groom themselves.
Writhing and frisking, turning and twisting
to fluff up their woolly coats.

When their fur is warmer than a thick, cosy blanket, the otters
are ready to nap. They float on the surface, bobbing on their backs.

Currents may carry them towards the land,
or out to the vast open sea, so some otters link
paws and drift together as a soft, snoring raft.

Overhead, a **magnificent frigatebird**
glides along. Like other birds, just half its brain
dozes at a time. It can soar for days, secretly sleeping
without needing to land on the water to rest.

In a wild and rocky North American canyon, something slips silently through the shadows of the towering pines.

A **mountain lion**, tired from her day of hunting, begins to climb. She squeezes between fallen boulders… scrambles up a rocky crag… crawls through an impossible space… and creeps into a mountainside cave.

There she hears the snores of her three speckled kittens, breathing softly, slowly, sound asleep.

Even sleeping lions need a bedroom to feel safe.

She snuggles up beside them, tucking her family into her tawny coat.

In a dry and dusty grassland of spiky leaves and spiny shrubs, an Australian **bearded dragon** climbs onto a stone that has been heated by the sun.

This resting reptile can't make her own body heat, but the warm rock will keep her toasty while she dozes.

The rock is like the lizard's very own hot water bottle!

Her eyelids start to flicker as she dozes off to sleep. Could this mean that dragon dreams are dancing through her head?

Even your garden may be full of sleeping animals.
Honeybees nap on the honeycomb in their
hives, resting their drooping head and wings.
But not all bees have a hive to call home.

Squash bees snuggle inside wilted
flowers, dozing until sunrise when the
petals open like orange stars.

Tent caterpillars weave
a silky bedroom in the branches of a tree.
After eating their fill of leaves, they crawl
inside to rest and hide.

Some **teddy bear bees** need no shelter at all.
These fuzzy, flying giants lock their strong jaws
around a sturdy stem. Then they hold on tight,
rocked to sleep by a night-time breeze.

Could **you** sleep inside a flower or halfway up a tree?
Bobbing in an ocean or standing on one leg?

Could you curl up on a toasty rock or doze inside a cave?
Hanging from a stalk of grass or balanced on a branch?

Or do you need a bedroom, and a bed that's warm and snug,
with a soft and fluffy pillow to rest your tired head?

No matter when or where you sleep,
it's never only you.
Somewhere bugs and sleeping lions
might be dreaming too.

More Secrets of Sleeping Animals

Scientists think that every animal sleeps, from the biggest whale to the tiniest fly. A sleeping animal's body is less active than usual, and they don't react to sights, sounds and smells like they would when awake. If disturbed, animals always try to catch up on missed sleep, as getting enough rest is very important.

Mallard duck

When you fall asleep, both sides of your brain rest at once. Mallard ducks can put just half of their brain to sleep, and therefore keep one eye open to spot danger. This is called unihemispheric sleep. Other animals, including pigeons, chickens, dolphins and fruit bats can be 'half asleep' too.

Giant panda

Giant pandas mainly eat bamboo, which is very low in energy. To save energy, pandas move slowly and nap often. Each nap lasts just two to four hours, before the panda gets so hungry it has to wake up and eat again! You can often tell where a panda has slept, because it leaves a pile of poo behind.

Meerkat

To survive cold desert nights, mobs of up to 50 meerkats dig around 20 underground sleeping burrows. At night, the group sleeps in a heap in one of the burrows. The mob moves every few days, so their bedrooms don't get too stinky!

Sociable weaver bird

Sociable weaver birds weave giant nests from dry grass, twigs and feathers. Each enormous nest is divided into hundreds of 'rooms'. By day, the weaver birds rest in the outside rooms to stay cool. At night, they roost in the central rooms, which stay warm even on freezing nights.

Caribbean flamingo

Flamingos forage for food at night if they get hungry, so they often sleep standing in water. Scientists have different ideas about why flamingos sleep on one leg – it might help keep them warm or it may just be more comfortable and stable.

Sperm whale

It's very hard to observe a sleeping whale! One team of scientists tracked a pod of sperm whales and found that they 'drift-dive' (rest with either their heads or tails pointing down) for an average of 12 minutes at a time, mostly in the evening or at night. Drift-diving whales seem to be sleeping, because they don't react to sounds – only to objects touching their skin.

Sea otter

Sea otters sleep in the water in 'rafts' of up to 100 otters. To avoid being washed away by ocean currents, they may link paws in pairs, or wrap themselves in long seaweed called kelp, to anchor themselves in place. Mothers hold their babies on their chests as they fall asleep, then slip below the water, leaving their baby bobbing on the surface.

Magnificent frigatebird

Frigatebirds sleep with just half their brain, which means they are able to rest as they fly! They can soar across the ocean for more than ten days without landing. Sometimes, the birds fall into a deeper sleep for a few seconds and fall towards the ocean, but they always wake up in time to flap to safety.

Mountain lion

A team of scientists visited almost 600 different 'bed sites' used by mountain lions in Yellowstone Park, USA and found that mountain lions often choose to sleep in places that are very hard to get to. Tall trees, lots of plants and rugged, steep slopes keep the sleeping lions safe from predators.

Bearded dragon

Humans dream during a special type of sleep called 'rapid eye movement' (REM) sleep. During REM sleep, our brains remain active and our eyelids flicker. Scientists have discovered that bearded dragons also experience REM sleep, which means they might dream too!

Western tent caterpillar

To stay safe from predators while they snooze, western tent caterpillars weave a 'tent' from silk that they make inside their bodies. The caterpillars use the tent more at night-time than in the day.

Western honeybee
Squash bee
Teddy bear bee

Sleeping bees become less active, their wings or antennae droop, and they don't respond as quickly to things around them. Honeybees sleep in their hives. While many female bees that live alone, such as teddy bear bees, sleep in their nests, male bees that live alone can often be spotted sleeping on or inside plants and flowers.